PIANO • VOCAL • GUITAR

THE BIG BOOK of

BLUES

Y0-CBB-980

Cover Photo: © Peter Amft

ISBN 978-1-4234-6787-8

HAL•LEONARD®
CORPORATION
7777 W. BLUEMOUND RD. P.O. BOX 13819 MILWAUKEE, WI 53213

Visit Hal Leonard Online at
www.halleonard.com

CONTENTS

AIN'T NOBODY'S BUSINESS

Words and Music by CLARENCE WILLIAMS, JAMES WITHERSPOON,
PORTER GRAINGER and ROBERT PRINCE

2. Me and my babe, __ oh, we fuss and fight
4. *(See additional lyrics)*

and then the next min - ute, ev - ery - thing is al - right, __

and it ain't no - bod - y's busi - ness what __ we do. __

Additional Lyrics

4. One day I think I'm going crazy,
   And the next day I'm laid back and lazy,
   And it ain't nobody's business if I do.
   To Verse 5

AS THE YEARS GO PASSING BY

Words and Music by
DEADRIC MALONE

1. There is noth-in' I can do,
3., 5. *Instrumental solo ad lib.*

as you leave me here to cry. _____

There is

noth-in' I can do, as you leave me here to cry. _____

BABY PLEASE DON'T GO

Words and Music by
JOSEPH LEE WILLIAMS

BEFORE YOU ACCUSE ME
(Take a Look at Yourself)

Words and Music by
ELLAS McDANIEL

Medium Shuffle

Be - fore you ac - cuse ___ me,
called your ___ ma - ma

take a look ___ at your - self. ___
'bout three or four nights ___ a - go. ___

Be - fore you ac - cuse ___ me,
I called your ___ ma - ma

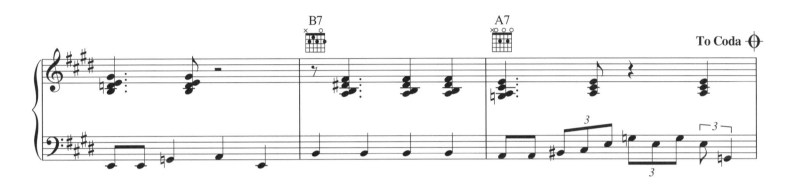

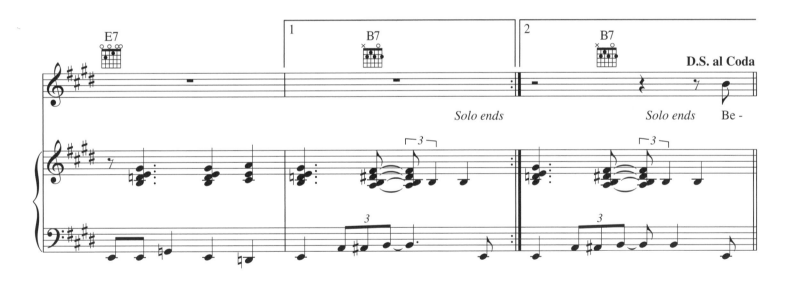

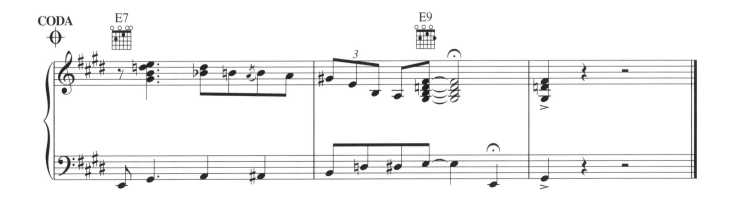

BIG BOSS MAN

Words and Music by AL SMITH
and LUTHER DIXON

got me work - ing, ba - by, work - ing 'round the
gon - na get a Boss Man, one that treats me
got me high, ba - by, got me wor - ried,

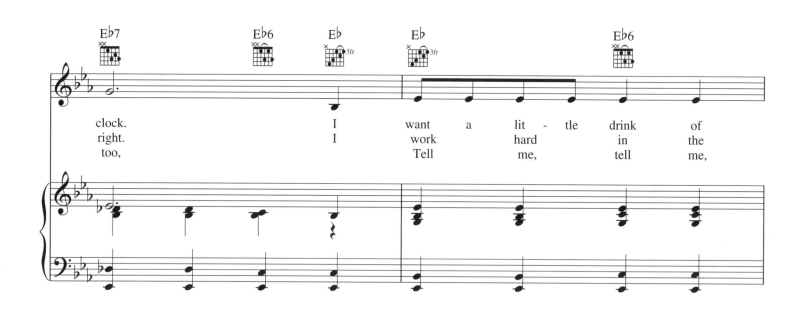

clock. I I want a lit - tle drink of
right. I work hard in the
too, Tell me, tell me,

wa - ter but you won't let Jim - my stop. Big Boss
day rest - ing at night. Big Boss
tell me what you're gon - na do? Big Boss

BLUES BEFORE SUNRISE

Words and Music by
LEROY CARR

THE BLUES IS ALRIGHT

Words and Music by
MILTON CAMPBELL

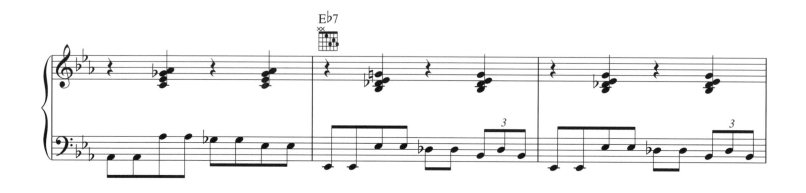

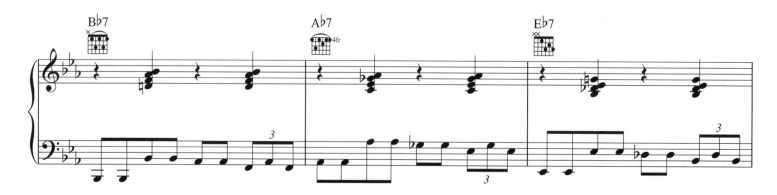

BLUES WITH A FEELING

Words and Music by
WALTER JACOBS

BRIGHT LIGHTS, BIG CITY

Words and Music by
JIMMY REED

wish you had lis - ten'd to some of the things _ that I say. _____

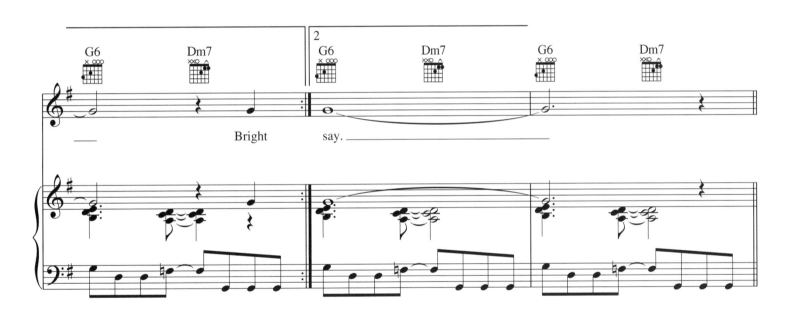

_____ Bright say. _____

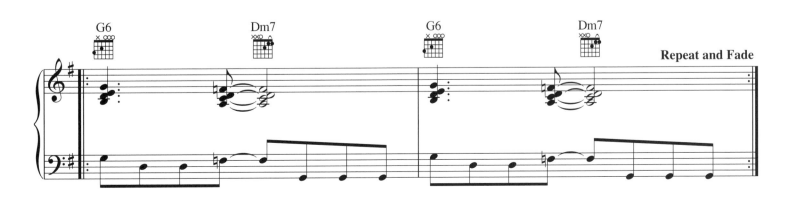

Repeat and Fade

BORN UNDER A BAD SIGN

Words and Music by BOOKER T. JONES
and WILLIAM BELL

When I was just a little boy, my daddy left home. He left me and my mama to go it all alone. You know, the times were hard, but somehow we survived. Lord knows, it's a mystery to me how she managed to keep us alive.

BOURGEOIS BLUES

Words and Music by HUDDIE LEDBETTER
Edited by ALAN LOMAX

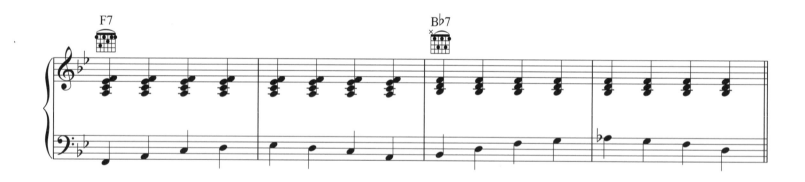

Me and my wife, _____ went all o - ver town. _____
Me and my wife, _____ we were stand - in' up - stairs. _____ I
Home of the brave, _____ land of the free, _____ I
Tell the col - ored folk to lis - ten to me. _____ Don't

CALDONIA
(What Makes Your Big Head So Hard?)

Words and Music by
FLEECIE MOORE

Medium Boogie-Woogie

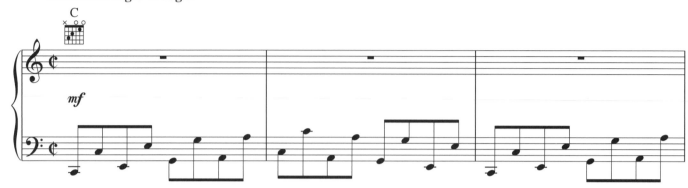

don - ia!   Cal - don - ia!   What makes your big head so   hard?

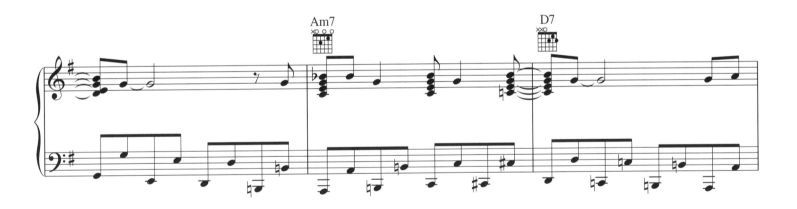

CATFISH BLUES

Words and Music by
ROBERT PETWAY

Additional Lyrics

6. Well, now I know, I know you don't want me.
   Why in the world won't you tell me so?
   Then I won't be caught, baby, 'round
   Your house no more,
   Your house no more,
   Your house no more.

CHEAPER TO KEEP HER

Words and Music by
MACK RICE

COME ON IN MY KITCHEN

Words and Music by
ROBERT JOHNSON

CRAZY BLUES

Words and Music by
PERRY BRADFORD

I'll tell you, folks, there ain't no change __ in me. __

My love __ for that { man __ / gal __ } will al - ways be. __

Now I can read { his / her } let - ters. I

sure can't read { his / her } mind. __

DIMPLES

Words and Music by JOHN LEE HOOKER
and JAMES BRACKEN

Moderate Shuffle

I love ___ the way you

walk,
day,
day,
jaws,

said I'm cra - zy 'bout your
in your neigh - bor -
walk - in' up and down the
you got dim - ples in your

walk.
hood,
street,
jaws,

I love _____ the way you
I see _____ you ev - 'ry
you got on your high heel
you got dim - ples in your

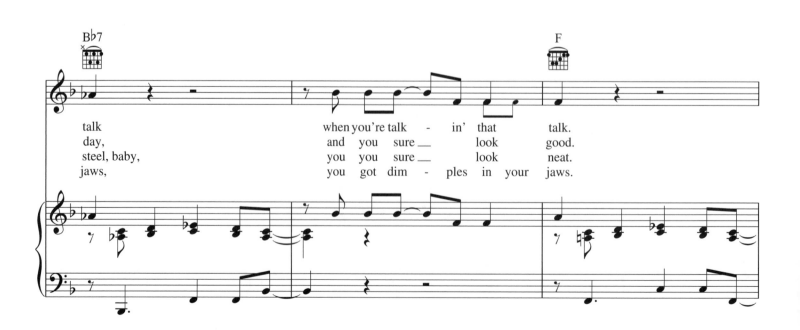

talk
day,
steel, baby,
jaws,

when you're talk - in' that talk.
and you sure _____ look good.
you you sure _____ look neat.
you got dim - ples in your jaws.

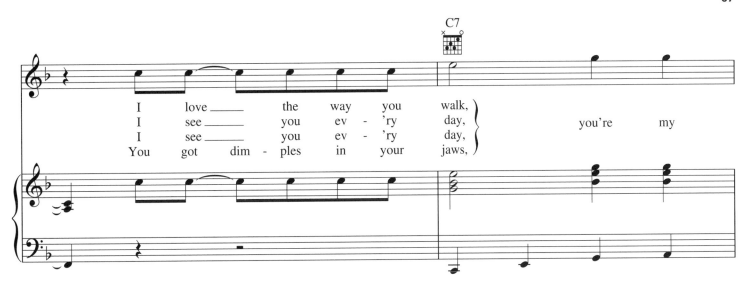

I love _____ the way you walk,
I see _____ you ev - 'ry day,
You got dim - ples in your jaws,

you're my

babe, I got my eyes on you.

I see _____ you ev - 'ry
I see _____ you ev - 'ry
You got dim - ples in your

you.

CROSSCUT SAW

Words and Music by
R.G. FORD

your log.
your log.
            I'll cut your
            I'll cut your

wood so eas - y for you,   you can't help ____ but say,
wood so eas - y for you,   you can't help ____ but say,

D.C. and Fade

"Hot Dog!"
"Hot Dog!"
           I've got a

EARLY IN THE MORNIN'

Words and Music by LEO HICKMAN,
LOUIS JORDAN and DALLAS BARTLEY

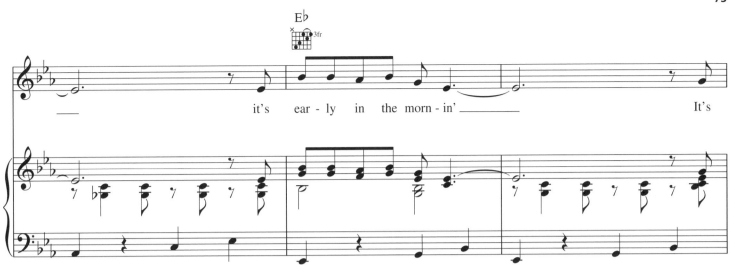

it's ear-ly in the morn-in' _____ It's

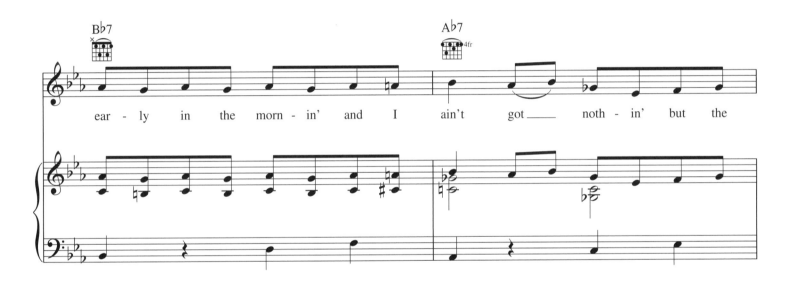

ear-ly in the morn-in' and I ain't got ____ noth-in' but the

blues _____ It's
I

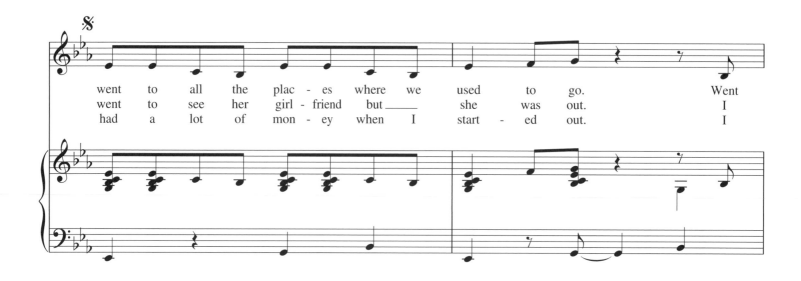

went to all the plac - es where we used to go. Went
went to see her girl - friend but____ she was out. I
had a lot of mon - ey when I start - ed out. I

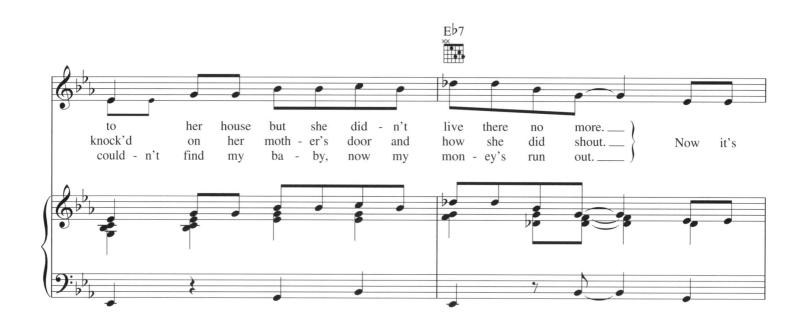

to her house but she did - n't live there no more.____ Now it's
knock'd on her moth - er's door and how she did shout.____ Now it's
could - n't find my ba - by, now my mon - ey's run out.____

Eb7

ear - ly in the morn - in'_____ it's

Ab7

ear - ly in the morn - in', _____ It's

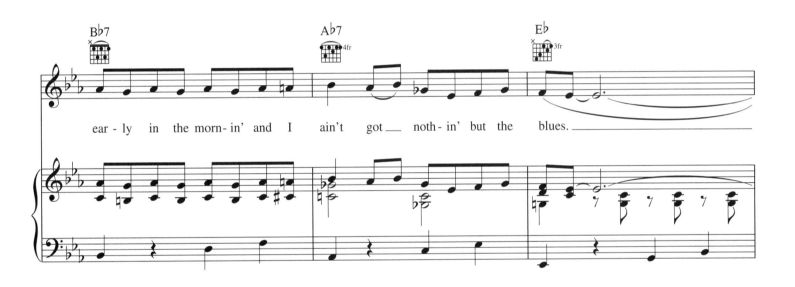

ear - ly in the morn - in' and I ain't got ___ noth - in' but the blues. _____

EASY BABY

Written by WILLIE DIXON

Lyrics:
Eas - y, ba - by, easy, ba - by.

Eas - y, ba - by, _ let me love _ you night and

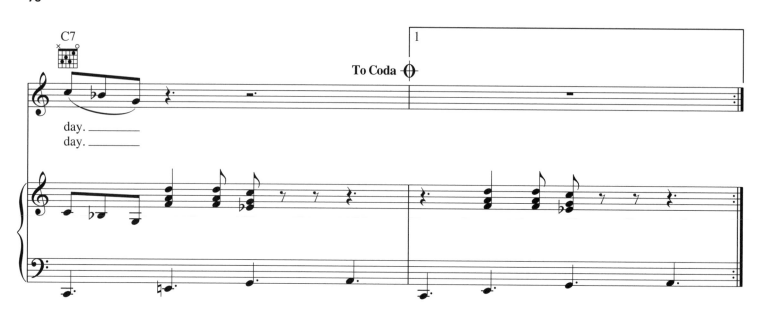

day.
day.

EVERYDAY I HAVE THE BLUES

Words and Music by
PETER CHATMAN

know I've had my ___ share. ___ I'm gon-na

pack my suit-case, ___ mov-in' on down the line, ___

___ oh, ___ I'm ___ gon-na pack my suit-case, move on down the

line; well, there ain't no-bod-y wor-ryin' and there ain't no-bod-y

FLIP, FLOP AND FLY

Words and Music by CHARLES CALHOUN
and LOU WILLIE TURNER

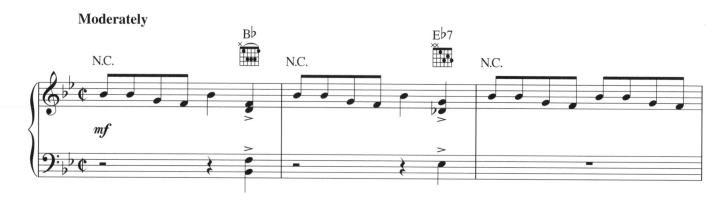

Now when I get the blues, I get me a rock-in' chair. _
one more kiss, hold it a long, long time. _

When I get the blues I
Give me one more kiss,

FORTY-FOUR

Words and Music by
CHESTER BURNETT

I done made my _____ shoul - der sore. _____
I don't know where in the world to go. _____

Well, I'm won - d'rin', ev - 'ry -
Well, I'm look - in' for me some

bod - y, where'd my ba - by go. _____
mon - ey. Pawned gun to have some gold. _____

Well, I'm so

GANGSTER OF LOVE

Words and Music by
JOHNNY WATSON

Moderately

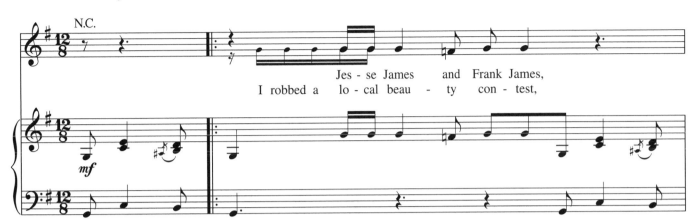

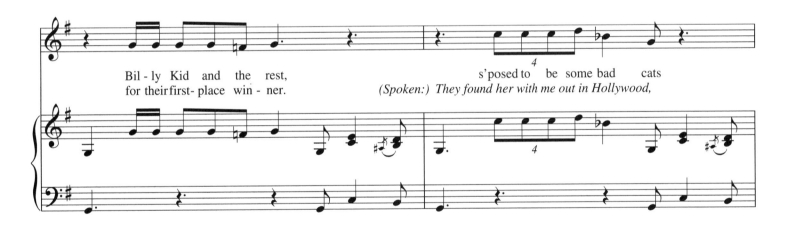

92

gang - ster of love. _____

gang - ster of love." _____

I jump on my white horse Cad - il - lac.

I ride a - cross the bor - der - line.

FURTHER ON UP THE ROAD

Words and Music by JOE VEASEY
and DON ROBEY

Fur - ther on up the road _____ some - bod - y's gon - na hurt you

Fur - ther on up the road _____ some - bod - y's gon - na hurt you

GOING DOWN SLOW

Words and Music by
J.B. ODEN

GOOD MORNING LITTLE SCHOOLGIRL

Words and Music by
WILLIE WILLIAMSON

Good morn - in', lit - tle school - girl.
know what,
air - plane.

Good morn - in', lit - tle school - girl.   Can I ___ come
some - times ___ I don't   know   what, ___   what in the world, ___
I'm gon - na buy me an   air - plane.   Fly ___ right

GOT MY MO JO WORKING

Words and Music by
PRESTON FOSTER

With a moving beat

I got my mo-jo work-ing but it just won't work __ on you.

I got my mo-jo work-ing but it

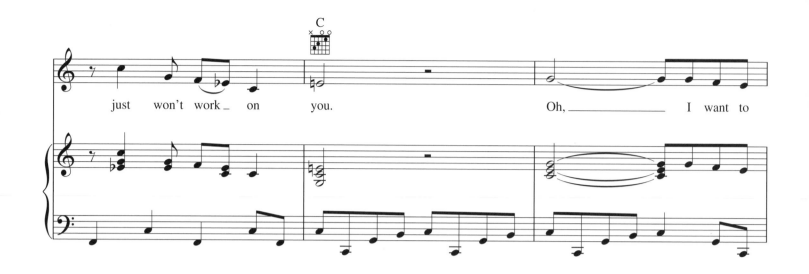

just won't work _ on you. Oh, _____ I want to

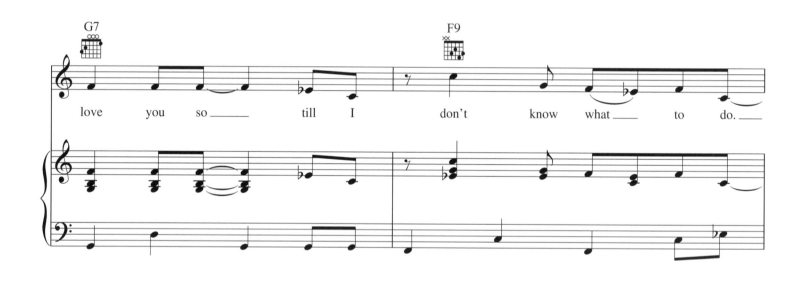

love you so _____ till I don't know what _____ to do. _____

Got my
I got a
I got my

HI-HEEL SNEAKERS

Words and Music by
ROBERT HIGGENBOTHAM

in case some fool may start a fight. _____
pret - ty soon you're gon - na knock 'em

(Hear what I say.) Put on your

dead. _____
(Hear what I say.)

HAVE YOU EVER LOVED A WOMAN

Words and Music by
BILLY MYLES

Slow Blues

1. Have you ev-er loved _ a wom-an
2.,3. (See additional lyrics)

so ___

much you trem-ble in pain? _

Have you ev-er loved _ a wom-an

so much

you trem - ble in pain?

And all the time, you know ___ she bears ___ an-oth-er

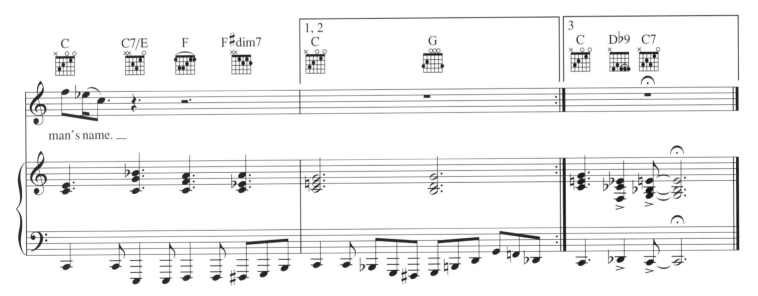

man's name. ___

Additional Lyrics

2. But you just love that woman so much, it's a shame and a sin.
   You just love that woman so much, it's a shame and a sin.
   But all the time, you know she belongs to your very best friend.

3. Have you ever loved a woman, oh, you know you can't leave her alone?
   Have you ever loved a woman, yes, you know you can't leave her alone?
   Something deep inside of you won't let you wreck your best friend's home.

HOW LONG, HOW LONG BLUES

Words and Music by
LEROY CARR

left me, _____ left me sing-in' those how _ long blues. _____

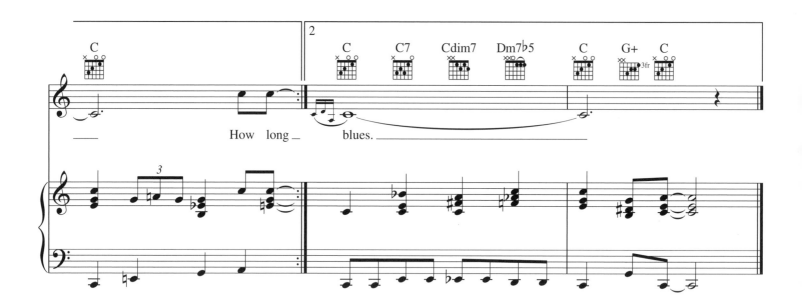

_____ How long _ blues. _____

Additional Choruses (ad lib.)

If I could holler like a Mountain Jack,
I'd go up on the mountain and call my baby back,
How long, how long, how long.

I went up to the mountain, looked as far as I could see,
The man (woman) had my woman (man) and the blues had poor me,
How long, how long, how long.

I can see the green grass growing on the hill,
But I ain't see the green grass on a dollar bill,
For so long, so long, baby so long.

If you don't believe I'm sinkin', see what a hole I'm in,
If you don't believe me, baby, look what a fool I've been,
Well, I'm gone how long, baby, how long.

I'm goin' down to Georgia, been up in Tennessee,
So look me over, baby, the last you'll see of me,
For so long, so long, baby so long.

The brook runs into the river, the river run into the sea,
If I don't run into my baby, a train is goin' to run into me,
How long, how long, how long.

I AIN'T GOT YOU

Words and Music by
CALVIN CARTER

Lyrics:

and no mat - ter where I goes, _____ you keep the

ring _____ in my nose, _____ but I ain't got you.

I got a tav - ern _____ and a li - quor store; _ I hit the

num - bers, _ four _____ for - ty - four. I got a mo - jo, _____

I JUST WANT TO MAKE LOVE TO YOU

Written by WILLIE DIXON

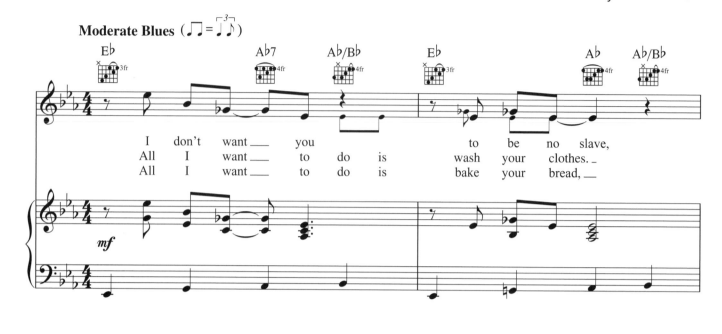

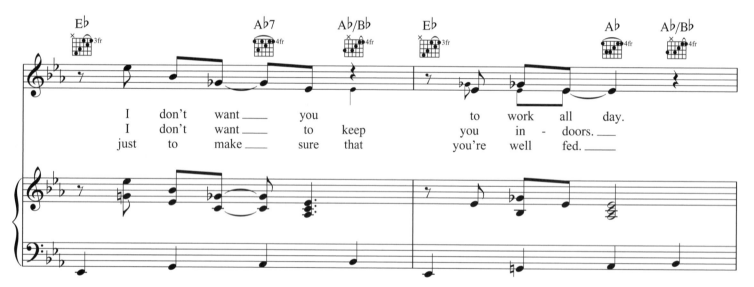

I KNOW WHAT YOU'RE PUTTIN' DOWN

Words and Music by LOUIS JORDAN
and BUD ALLEN

I'D RATHER GO BLIND

Words and Music by ELLINGTON JORDAN
and BILLY FOSTER

Some-thing told me _____ it was o - ver _____

when I saw you _ and her talk - ing. _____

I'M A MAN

Words and Music by
ELLAS McDANIEL

I'M READY

Written by
WILLIE DIXON

Shuffle Blues

I am read - y, _____ read - y as an - y - bod - y can be.

I am read - y, _____

read - y as an - y - bod - y can be. _____ I am

read-y for you. __ I hope you're read-y for me. ____

I got an ax-han-dle pis-tol on a grave-yard frame that shoots

pret-ty lit-tle chicks with your cur-ly hair.

drink-in' gin __ like nev-er be-fore. I

tomb-stone bul-lets wear-in' balls and chains. __ I'm drink-in' T. N. T. I'm smok-in'

Know you feel like I ain't no-where. __ But stop what you're doin', ba-by,

feel so good, I want you to know. __ One more drink, I

KANSAS CITY

Words and Music by JERRY LEIBER
and MIKE STOLLER

Medium Blues

I'm go-in' to Kan - sas Cit - y,___ Kan - sas Cit - y here I

come._____ I'm go-in' to Kan - sas Cit - y,___

Kan - sas Cit - y here I come._____ They got a

IF YOU LOVE ME LIKE YOU SAY

Words and Music by
LITTLE JOHNNY TAYLOR

If you love me like you say,

why you treat me like you do?

If you love me like you say, ba - by,

IT HURTS ME TOO

Words and Music by
MEL LONDON

Slow Blues

You say you're hurt, _____ you al - most lost your

mind, the man you love, _____ he hurt you all the

time, when things go wrong, go wrong with

JUKE

Words and Music by
WALTER JACOBS

KEY TO THE HIGHWAY

Words and Music by BIG BILL BROONZY
and CHAS. SEGAR

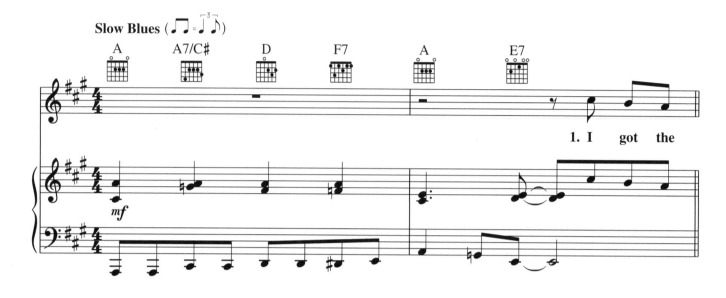

Additional Lyrics

2. I'm goin' back to the border
    Where I'm better known.
    Though you haven't done nothin',
    Drove a good man away from home.

3. Oh, gimme one more kiss, mama,
    Just before I go,
    'Cause when I leave this time,
    I won't be back no more.

4. *Repeat Verse 1*

KIDNEY STEW BLUES

Words and Music by LEONA BLACKMAN
and EDDIE VINSON

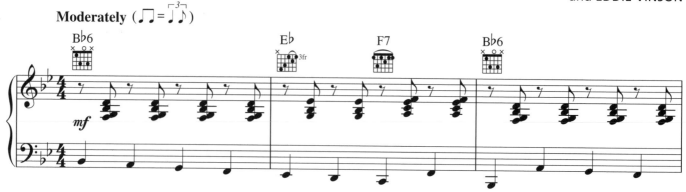

KOZMIC BLUES

Words and Music by JANIS JOPLIN
and GABRIEL MEKLER

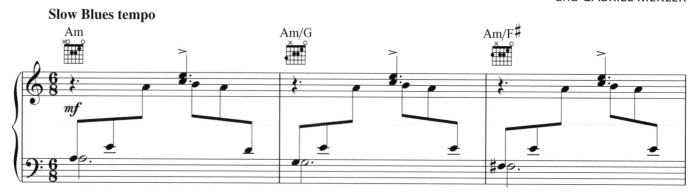

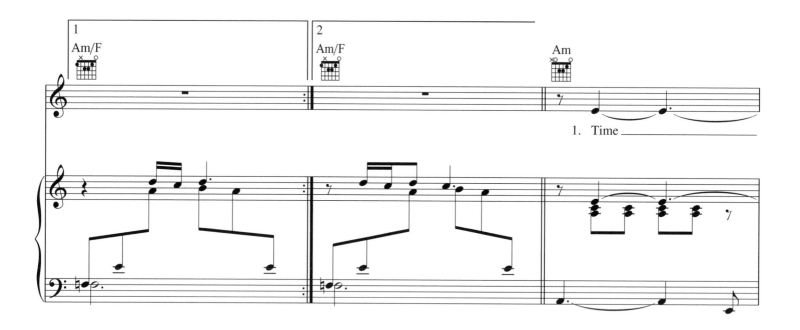

1. Time _____

keeps mov-in' on, _____

2. Dawn _____ has come at last, _____
3. (See additional lyrics)

twen-ty-five years, hon-ey, in just

one night, __ oh, yeah. ____ Well, I'm twen-ty-five years

dif-f'rence, babe, ___ I bet-ter hold it now, _ I'm gon-na need it, yeah. _

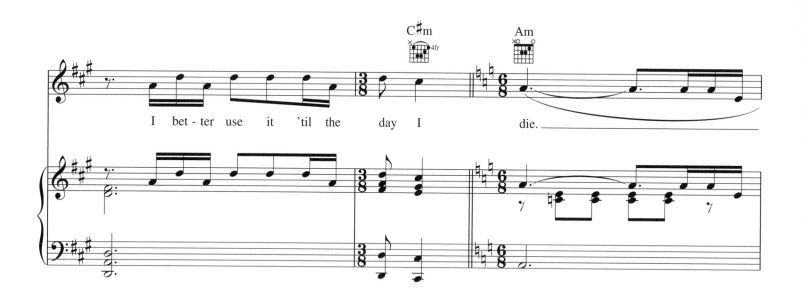

I bet-ter use it 'til the day I die. ___

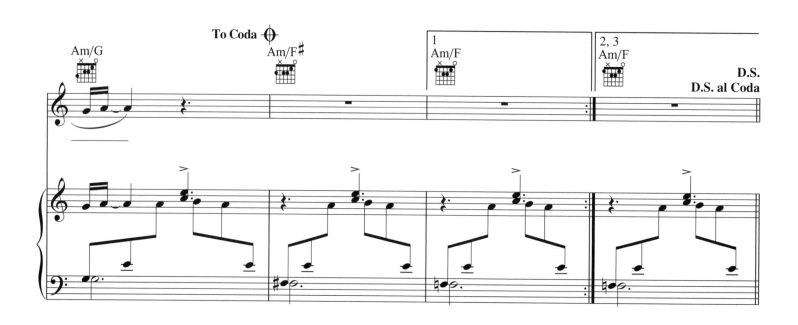

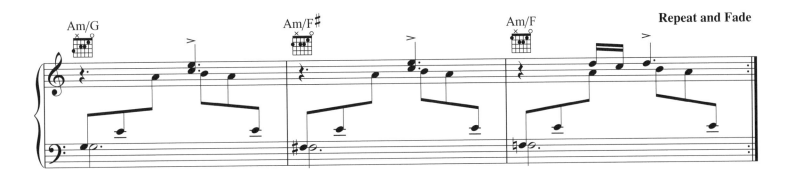

Additional Lyrics

3. Don't expect any answers, dear
    For, I know that they don't come with age, no, no
    They ain't never gonna love you any better, babe
    And they're never gonna love you right
    So you better dig it right now, right now, oh.

Chorus 2
Well, it don't make no diff'rence, babe
And I know, that I can always try
Well, there's a fire inside ev'ry one of us
You're gonna need it now,
I get to hold it, yeah
I'm gonna use it, 'till the day I die.

Chorus 3
Don't make no diff'rence, babe, no, no, no
And it never, ever will
I wanna talk about livin', and lovin', yeah
I get to hold it, babe
I'm gonna need it now,
I'm gonna use it..

Chorus 4
Don't make no diff'rence, babe
Oh, honey, I hate to be the one
I said, you better live your life
And, you better love your life
Oh babe, some day you're gonna have to cry
Yes indeed, yes, indeed.

THE LEMON SONG

Words and Music by CHESTER BURNETT, JOHN BONHAM,
JIMMY PAGE, ROBERT PLANT and JOHN PAUL JONES

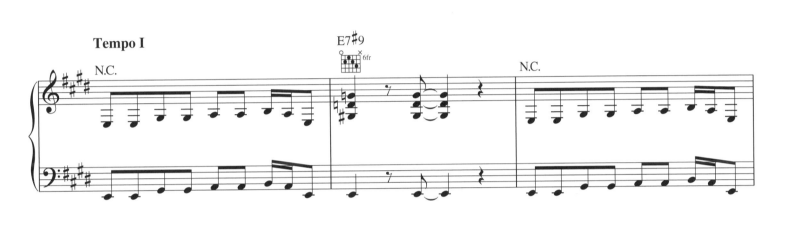

Tempo I

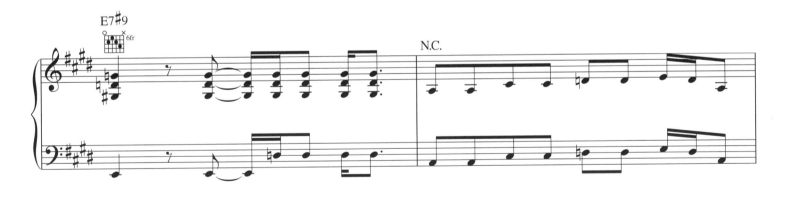

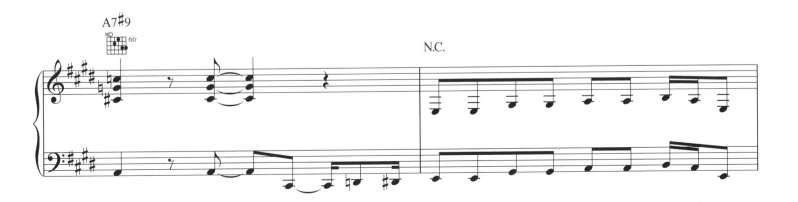

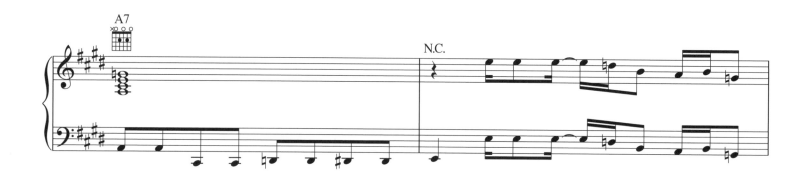

I went to sleep last night. _

I worked as hard as I can. _   I bring home my mon-ey, you take it and

give it to an-oth-er man. _ I should-'ve quit you, ba - by,

such a long time a - go.

I would-n't be here with all my trou-bles down on this kill- in' floor. _

Squeeze me, babe, till the juice runs down my

leg. ___

Squeeze me, ba - by, till the juice runs down ___ my

leg.

LET THE GOOD TIMES ROLL

Words and Music by SAM THEARD
and FLEECIE MOORE

Moderate Blues

Hey, ev-'ry-bod-y, let's have some fun. You on-ly live but once, __ and when you're dead you're done. __ Let the

LET'S HAVE A NATURAL BALL

Words and Music by
ALBERT KING

Recorded a half step lower.

Well, come on, ba - by, let's have a nat - 'ral

LITTLE RED ROOSTER

Written by WILLIE DIXON

fight-ing a-mong them-selves. ___
please send him home. ___

He
I

don't want no hens in the barn - yard
had no peace in the barn - yard

lay-ing eggs for no-bod-y
since ___ the red roost-er's been

else.
gone.

Now if you

LOVE STRUCK BABY

Written by STEVIE RAY VAUGHAN

Fast Rock 'N Roll

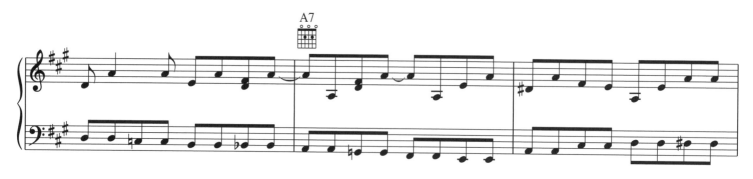

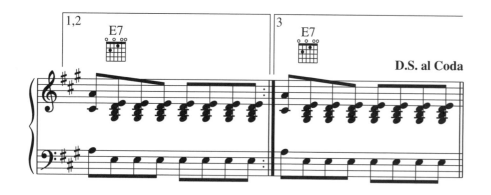

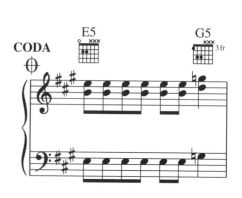

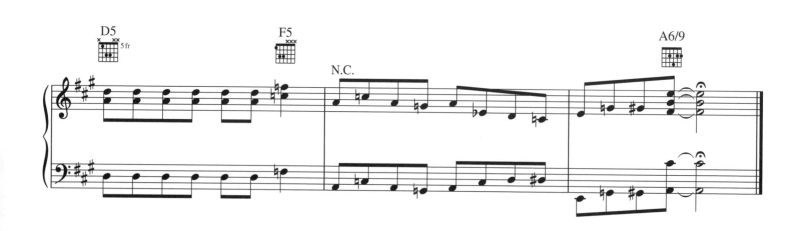

MATCHBOX

Words and Music by
CARL LEE PERKINS

Bright Shuffle

I said I'm sit-tin' here __ watch-in', match-box hole in my clothes; __

I said I'm sit-tin' here won-d'rin', (watch-in')

match-box hole in my clothes.

I

MARY HAD A LITTLE LAMB

Written by BUDDY GUY

Moderately

it.

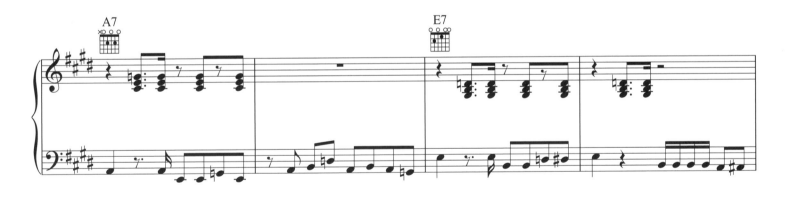

MEMPHIS BLUES

Words and Music by
W.C. HANDY

Moderate Blues

You want to be my man,— you got to give me for-ty dol-lars

down.   You want to be my man,— you'll give me

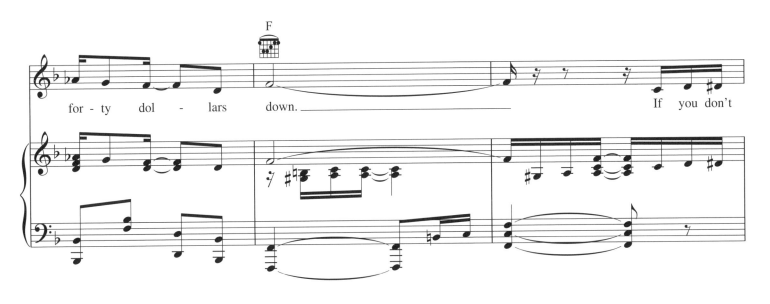

for - ty dol - lars down. _____ If you don't

be my man, __ your ba - by's gon - na shake this town. _____

You want to __ Mis - ter Crump don't 'low __ no
Crump don't 'low __ it,

eas - y rid - ers here,
ain't goin' have __ it here,

Crump don't 'low __ no eas - y rid - ers here.)
Crump don't 'low __ it, ain't goin' have __ it here.)

We don't care __ what Mis - ter Crump don't 'low __

THE MIDNIGHT SPECIAL

New Words and New Music Adaptation by HUDDIE LEDBETTER
Collected and Adapted by JOHN A. LOMAX and ALAN LOMAX

Medium Rock

You get us in the morn - in' ___   you hear the ding - dong
Hous - ton, ___   you'd bet - ter walk on
Lu - cy ___   how in the world do you

ring.   Now you look ___ up - on a   ta - ble
by.   Oh, you'd bet - ter not gam - ble,   boy, ___
know?   I know by her a - pron and   by

you see the same damn_ thing.
I say you'd bet - ter not fight.
the dress that she _ wore,

You find no food up - on that
Well now, the sher - iff, he'll grab
an um - brel - la on her shoul-

ta - ble _ noth - ing _ up in the pan. _
you and _ his boys _ will pull you down. _
der, _____ a piece of pa - per in her hand.

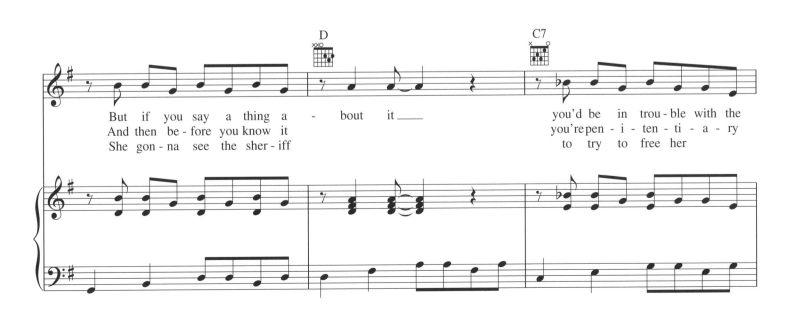

But if you say a thing a - bout it _
And then be - fore you know it
She gon - na see the sher - iff

you'd be in trou - ble with the
you're pen - i - ten - ti - a - ry
to try to free her

MILK COW BLUES

Words and Music by
KOKOMO ARNOLD

when you won't do right your - self?

How can I do right, ba - by,

when you won't do right your - self?

If my good gal quits me,

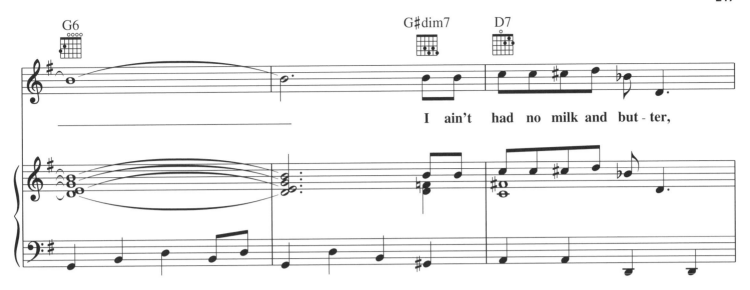

I ain't had no milk and but-ter,

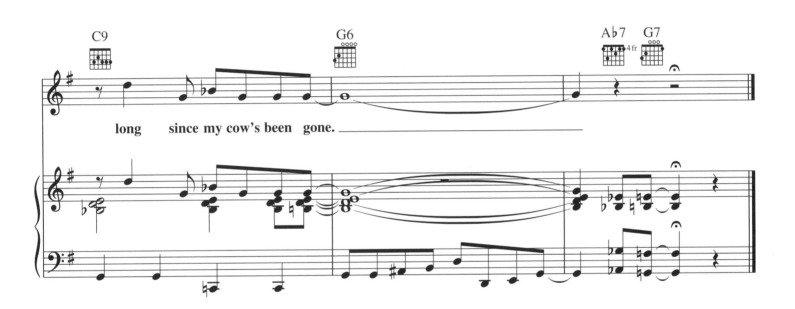

long since my cow's been gone.

Additional Lyrics

My blues fell this mornin' and my love came falling down,
My blues fell this mornin' and my love came falling down,
I may be a low-down dog, mama, but please don't dog me around.

It takes a rockin' chair to rock, a rubber ball to roll,
Takes a long, tall, sweet gal to satisfy my soul,
Lord, I don't feel welcome, no place I go,
'Cause the woman I love done throwed me from her door.

MY BABE

Written by WILLIE DIXON

NIGHT TIME IS THE RIGHT TIME

Words and Music by ROOSEVELT SYKES
and JAMES ODEN

NOBODY KNOWS YOU WHEN YOU'RE DOWN AND OUT

Words and Music by
JIMMIE COX

I once lived the life of a mil-lion-aire,_ spend-ing my mon-ey, I did-n't care,_ al-ways tak-ing my friends out for a good time,_ buy-ing cham-pagne,_ gin and wine._ But

ORGAN GRINDER BLUES

Words and Music by
CLARENCE WILLIAMS

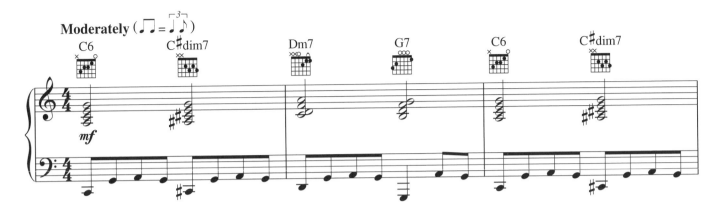

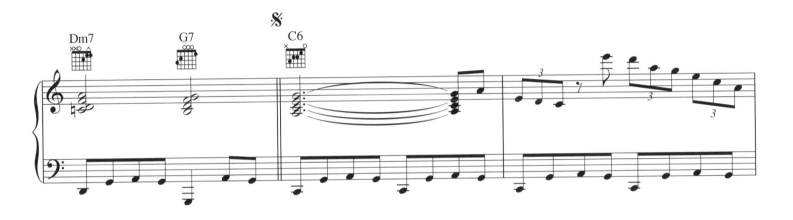

To Coda ⊕

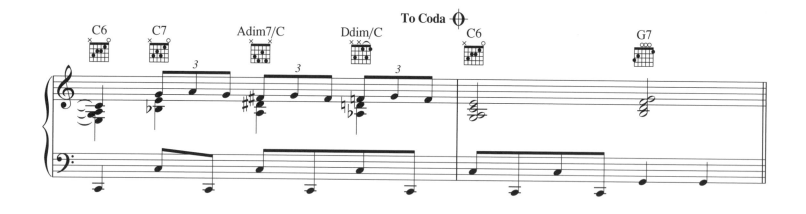

Or - gan grind - er,

PARCHMAN FARM BLUES

Written and Composed by
BUKKA WHITE

1. Judge   gim - me
2. Oh,
3.-5. *(See additional lyrics)*

life   this   morn - in'   down   on ____
good - bye, wife.   Oh,   you ____

Parch - man   Farm. ____
have ____ done   gone. ____

Judge ____ gim - me life this morn - in'
Oh, _____ good - bye, wife. ____

down ____ on Parch - man Farm. I would - n't
Oh, ____ you have done gone. But I

hate it so bad, but I left my
hope some - day you will hear my

wife ____ in mourn - in'. _____
lone - some song. _____

Additional Lyrics

3. Oh you, listen you men
   I don't mean no harm
   Oh-oh listen you men
   I don't mean no harm
   If you wanna do good
   You better stay off old Parchman Farm, yeah.

4. We go to work in the mo'nin
   Just a-dawn of day
   We go to work in the mo'nin
   Just a-dawn of day
   Just at the settin' of the sun
   That's when da work is done, yeah.

5. Ooh, I'm down on old Parchman Farm
   I sho' wanna go back home, yeah
   I'm down on the old Parchman Farm
   But I sho' wanna go back home, yeah
   But I hope someday I will overcome.

PLEASE SEND ME SOMEONE TO LOVE

Words and Music by
PERCY MAYFIELD

Slow Blues

Hea - ven, ___ please send ___ to all man - kind, ___ un - der - stand - ing ___ and ___ peace of mind. ___ But, if it's not ask - ing too much, ___

RECONSIDER BABY

Words and Music by
LOWELL FULSON

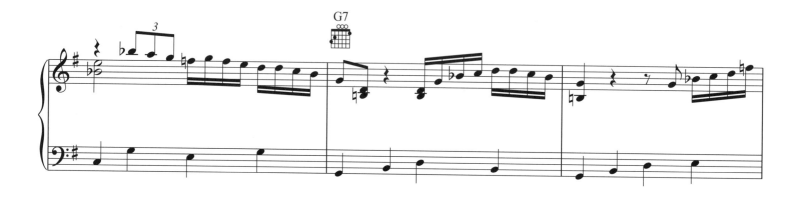

THE RIGHT TIME

Words and Music by
LEW HERMAN

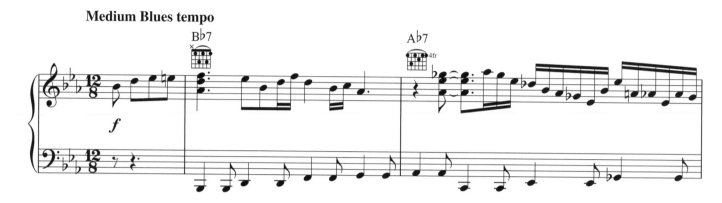

You know the

night time, dar-lin',   is the right time _____   to be _____
moth-er, now,   hadn't a dime, now. _____   My fa-

SEE SEE RIDER

Words and Music by
MA RAINEY

SATURDAY NIGHT FISH FRY

Words and Music by ELLIS WALSH
and LOUIS JORDAN

Solid beat tempo

Now if you've ev - er been down to New Or - leans___ then you can
bud - dy and me was on the main stem,_____

un - der - stand___ just what I mean.___ Now all thru the week it's
fool - in' 'round___ just me and him.___ We de - cid - ed we could use a lit - tle

rock- in'. You nev - er see such scuf- flin' and

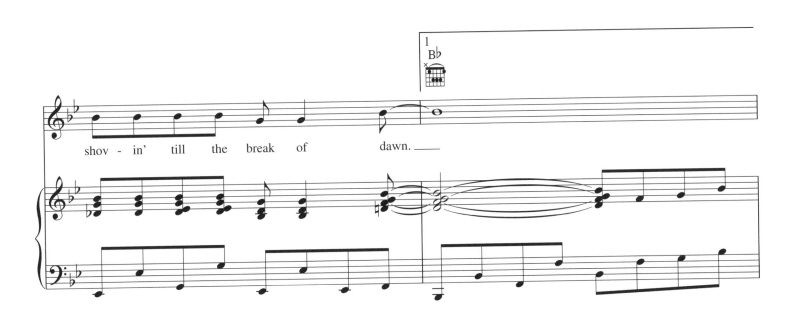

shov - in' till the break of dawn. ___

Now my ___

SITTING ON TOP OF THE WORLD

Words and Music by
CHESTER BURNETT

SMOKESTACK LIGHTNING

Words and Music by
CHESTER BURNETT

Moderately

N.C.

mf

Cm

Smoke, _____ smoke - stack light - ning,
_____ tell me, ba - by,
_____ tell me, ba - by,

shin - ing just like gold. _____ Well,
what's the mat - ter here? _____ Well,
where did you stay last night? _____ Well,

don't you hear me cry - ing, boo -
don't you hear me cry - ing, boo -
don't you hear me cry - ing, boo -

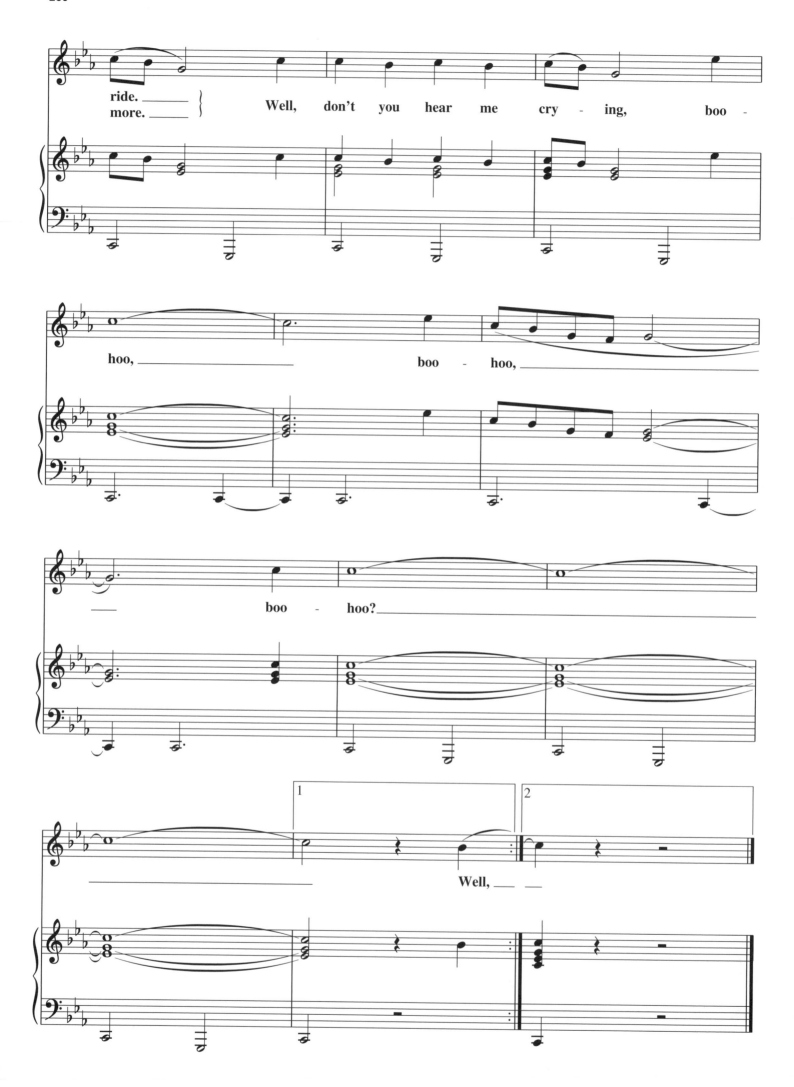

SMOKING GUN

Written by BRUCE BROMBERG,
RICHARD COUSINS and ROBERT CRAY

Moderately

I get a con-stant bus - y sig - nal   when I
May - be you want to end ___ it.   You've had your
Instrumental solo
stand - ing here ___ be - wil - dered.   I can't re -

call you on ___ the phone. ___   I get a strong un-eas - y feel
fill of my ___ kind of fun.   But you don't know how ___ to tell ___
mem - ber just what I've done. ___   I can hear the si - rens whin -

- ing,   you're not sit - ting there ___ a - lone. ___   I'm hav - in'
___ me,   and you know that I'm not that dumb. ___   I put
- ing,   my eyes blind - ed by ___ the sun. ___   I

STATESBORO BLUES

Words and Music by
WILLY McTELL

Solo ends   Well, my

ma - ma died and left me,   my pa - pa died and left me.   I   ain't good look-in', ba - by,   but I'm

Additional Lyrics

2. I woke up this mornin', and I had them Statesboro blues.
   I woke up this mornin', and I had them Statesboro blues.
   Well, I looked over in the corner, baby.
   Your grandpa seem to have them, too.

3. I love that woman better than any woman I've ever seen.
   Well, I love that woman better than any woman I've ever seen.
   Well, she treat me like a king, yeah, yeah, yeah.
   I treat her like a doggone queen.

SUGAR MAMA

Words and Music by
JOHN LEE HOOKER

Sug-ar ma-ma, sug-ar ma-ma.

Sug-ar ma-ma, please come back to me. Sug-ar

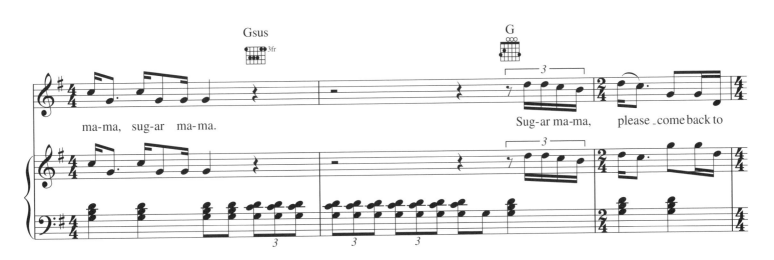

ma-ma, sug-ar ma-ma. Sug-ar ma-ma, please come back to

ma - ma, I sure___ can hear your name. _____

The rea-son I'm cra - zy 'bout you,

Gsus   G   Gsus   G

sug - ar ma - ma,   be-cause you ease _____ my

wor-ried mind. ___

I like my cof-fee sweet ear-ly in the morn-in'.

You know I'm cra-zy 'bout my tea at night.

(Spoken:) You know what I mean about that, sugar mama.

I like my

TEN LONG YEARS

Words and Music by RILEY B. KING
and JULES BIHARI

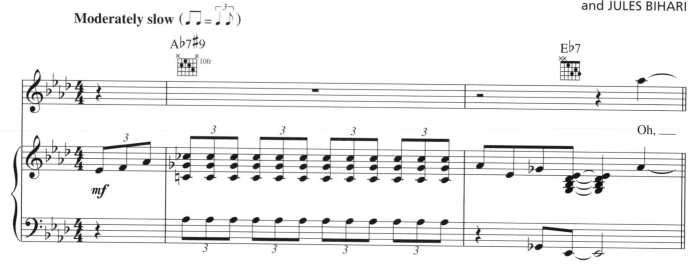

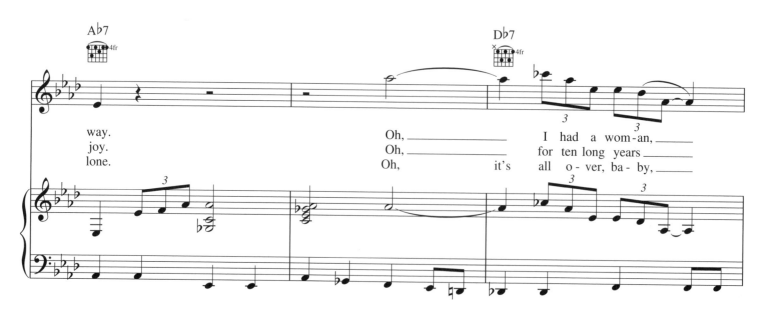

THE THINGS THAT I USED TO DO

Words and Music by
EDDIE "GUITAR SLIM" JONES

Moderately slow

1. Things that I used to do,
3. *Instrumental solo ad lib.*

Lord, I won't do no

more.

The

things that I used to do, Lord, I won't do no more.

Additional Lyrics

4. I'm goin' to send you back to your mama, darlin'. Lord, I'm goin' back to my family, too.
   I'm goin' to send you back to your mama, darlin'. Lord, I'm goin' back to my family, too.
   Nothin' I can do to please you, darlin'.
   Oh, I just can't get along wit' you.

THREE HOURS PAST MIDNIGHT

Words and Music by JOHNNY WATSON
and SAUL BIHARI

1. It is

three hours __ past mid-night and my __ ba-by's no-where a - round.

2.,3. *(See additional lyrics)*

Yes, _____ three hours __ past mid-night and my ba-by's no-where a -

round. ___   Well, I lis-ten so   hard ____ to hear her foot-steps.

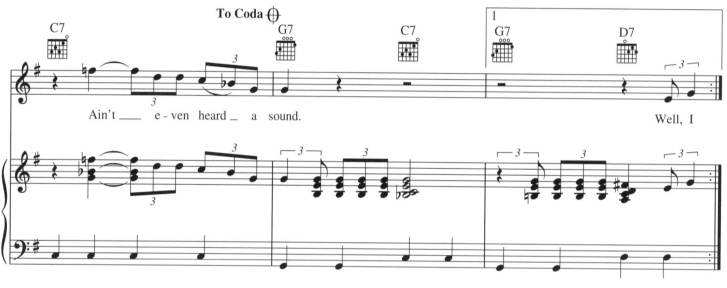

Ain't ____ e - ven heard __ a sound.   Well, I

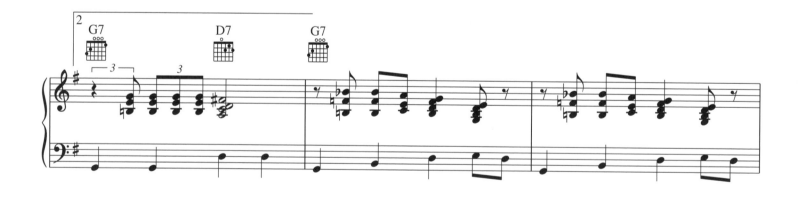

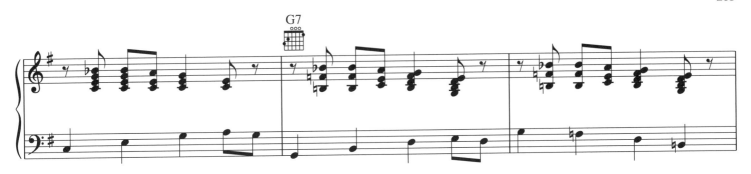

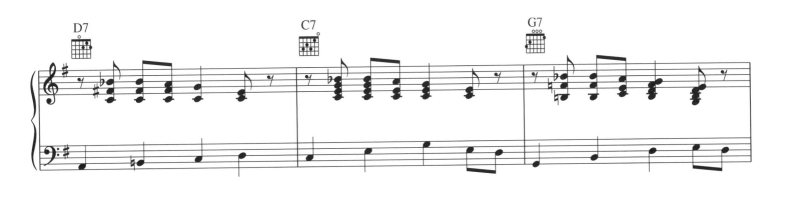

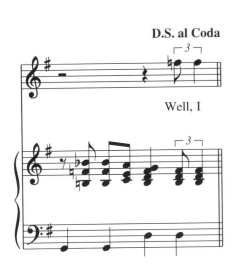

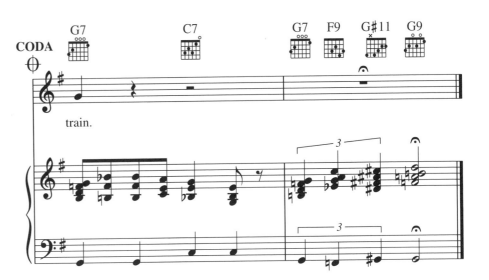

Additional Lyrics

2. Well, I toss and tumble on my pillow, but I just can't close my eyes.
Well, I toss and tumble on my pillow, but I just can't close my eyes.
If my baby don't come back pretty soon,
Yes, I just can't be satisfied.

3. Well, I tried so hard to take it, but my baby's drivin' me insane.
Well, I tried so hard to take it, but my baby's drivin' me insane.
Well, if she don't come back pretty soon,
Yes, gonna catch that midnight train.

THIRD DEGREE

Written by WILLIE DIXON
and EDDIE BOYD

THE THRILL IS GONE

Words and Music by ROY HAWKINS
and RICK DARNELL

The thrill has gone a - way _ from me.
I'm free _____ from your _____ spell.

Al - though I'll _____ still live on, _____ but so _____
And now that _____ it's all o - ver, all I can

lone - ly _____ I'll _____ be.
do _____ is _____ wish you   well.

WANG DANG DOODLE

Written by WILLIE DIXON

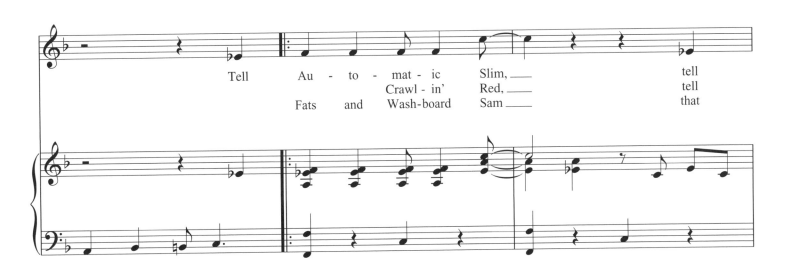

Tell Au - to - mat - ic Slim, _____ tell
Crawl - in' Red, _____ tell
Fats and Wash - board Sam _____ that

Ra - zor Tot - in' Jim. _____ Tell Butch - er Knife Tot - in' An -
Ab - ys - sin - ian Ned. _____ Go tell ol' _____ Pis - tol Pete _
ev - 'ry - bod - y gon' _____ jam. _____ Tell Shak - in' Box - car Joe _

TROUBLE IN MIND

Words and Music by
RICHARD M. JONES

TUPELO
(Tupelo Blues)

Words and Music by
JOHN LEE HOOKER

THIS MELODY CONTINUES UNDER NARRATION

Did you read about the flood? It happened long time ago,
A little country town way back in Mississippi.
It rained and it rained, it rained both night and day.
The poor people got worried, they began to cry,
"Lord have mercy, where can we go now?"

There were women and there was children screaming and crying,
"Lord have mercy and a great disaster,
Who can we turn to now, but you?"
The great flood of Tupelo, Mississippi.

It happened one evening, one Friday evening a long time ago,
It rained and it started raining.
The people of Tupelo, out on the farm gathering their harvest,
A dark cloud rolled back in Tupelo, Mississippi. Hm Hm

TURN ON YOUR LOVE LIGHT

Words and Music by DON ROBEY
and JOE SCOTT

YOU SHOOK ME

Words and Music by WILLIE DIXON
and J.B. LENOIR

Slow Blues

(Spoken:) Mm mm.

You know you shook   me, ba - by.
                                me, ba - by,

You've Got to Love Her With a Feeling

By FREDDIE KING
and SONNY THOMPSON